WEST GATE ELEMENTARY
8031 URBANNA ROAD
MANASSAS, VA 20109

NIGHT WONDERS

JANE ANN PEDDICORD

ini Charlesbridge

Beside a dark and quiet sea
beneath a starlit canopy,
I shone my light upon a star
and wondered, *What is out that far?*

Ascending high across the sky
as if inviting me to fly,
the light escaped the Earth's embrace
and soared away through open space.

Light moves in a straight line at 186,000 miles per second.
It travels on and on forever, unless it hits something. Our sky
is filled with specks of dust and water that can slow down, stop,
or turn aside rays of light. But outer space is very empty. Once a
light beam makes it through Earth's crowded atmosphere, there
is little to stop it from reaching the stars.

I wished that night with all my might
that I might stow aboard that flight
and sail upon the wings of light
across the sparkling winds of night.

I stared at that enchanting view
until my daring dream came true
and I was gliding by the face
that welcomes us to outer space.

The Moon has hardly changed for three billion years. But when the solar system was young, huge rocks from space blasted deep craters in the Moon's surface, and hot lava bubbled up through its crust. The flowing lava hardened into dark, dry plains that look like eyes and a lopsided grin from Earth. Now, only passing pebbles dent the Moon's familiar face.

Advancing past a brilliant glare
I saw, by luck, a solar flare,
exploding flames across the sky
one hundred million meters high.

The Sun is a churning ball of blazing hot gas, so big that it weighs two billion, billion, billion tons. Its tremendous weight forces the tiny atoms deep in its core to fuse, or join together, releasing energy that lights and warms the solar system. Sometimes, energy gets trapped in tornado-like storms on the Sun's surface. But eventually, it bursts free in a brilliant, fiery fountain called a solar flare.

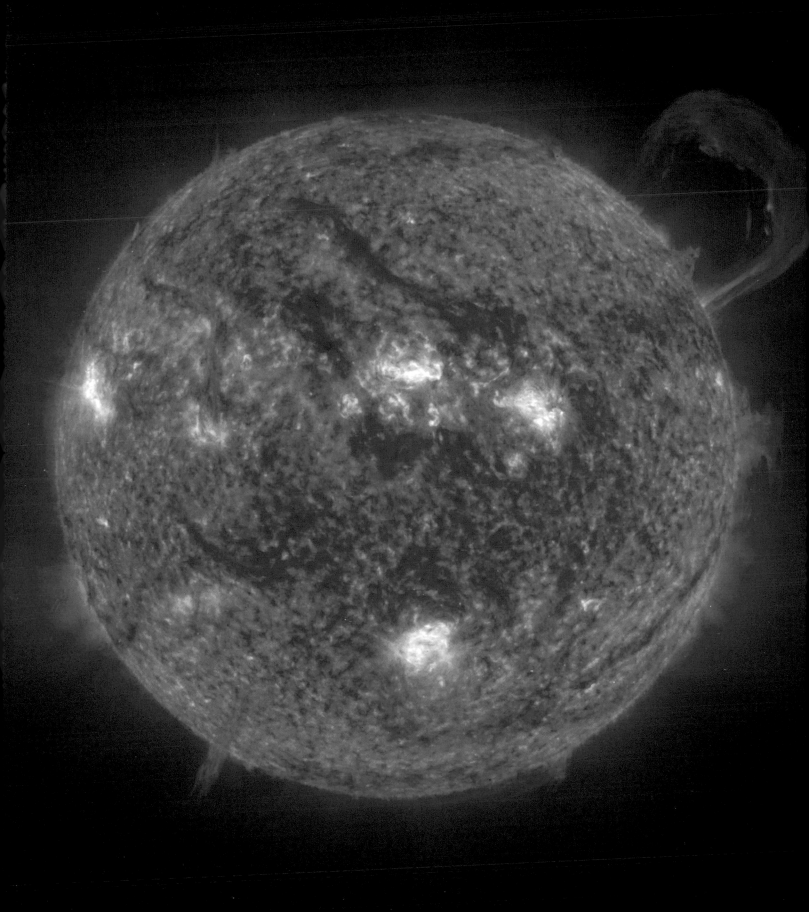

I passed the planets one by one
revolving round the glowing Sun,
then sped through empty space so far
our Sun looked like a distant star . . .

Scientists think that the solar system formed from a great, spinning disc
of gas and dust. The Sun grew out of the thick, hot center of the disc
and the planets from the cooler, outer bands. The inner planets —
Mercury, Venus, Earth, and Mars — formed into rocky spheres. Jupiter,
Saturn, Uranus, and Neptune spun into giant gas balls. Tiny Pluto, once
considered the ninth planet, is simply a very large ice ball at the far edge
of the solar system.

Neptune

Uranus

Saturn

Jupiter

Mars

Earth

Venus

Mercury

Sun

Planet sizes are to scale but distances are not.

Like one of many grains of sand
sprinkled on a velvet band,
each turning nighttime into day
and lighting up the Milky Way.

Our Sun is one of around 400 billion stars in a spinning, pancake-shaped group of stars called the Milky Way galaxy. When we look toward the center of the pancake from Earth, we see a hazy band of white across the night sky. Dark ribbons running through the band are vast dust clouds, blocking our view. Each point of light is a star that, like our Sun, lights and warms its solar neighborhood.

I flew upon my steady beam

to lands more distant than a dream,

where stars are born, and live, and die,

in diamond veils called nebulae.

Nebulae (NEB-yoo-lie) are enormous, swirling pools of dust and gas.
Deep inside a nebula, bits of matter pull together into clumps.
Sometimes a clump grows so dense that it collapses inward, squeezing
the matter in its core into a tight, hot ball. If the matter is packed
tightly enough, atoms begin to fuse together, releasing energy. The
energy escapes in fiery eruptions that turn the clump of dust into a
star. The newborn star lights up the surrounding dust and glitters
brightly through the ghostly nebula.

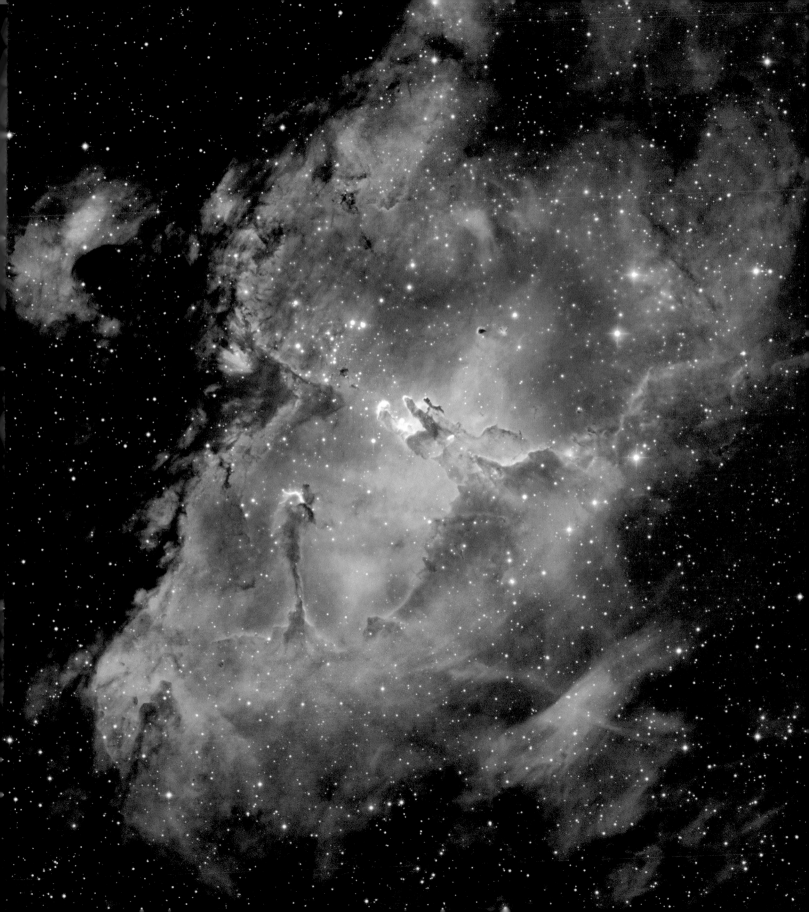

And then we happened, just by chance,

to pass an interstellar dance,

a red star swinging round a blue

with streams of gas between the two.

Nebulae often give birth to twins. In fact, nearly half of the "stars" in our night sky are actually twins, or even triplets, held together by the pull of gravity. Twin stars circle each other like dancers holding hands. The closer the stars are, the faster they will spin, and the more likely it is that their gases will stream together in a giant figure 8.

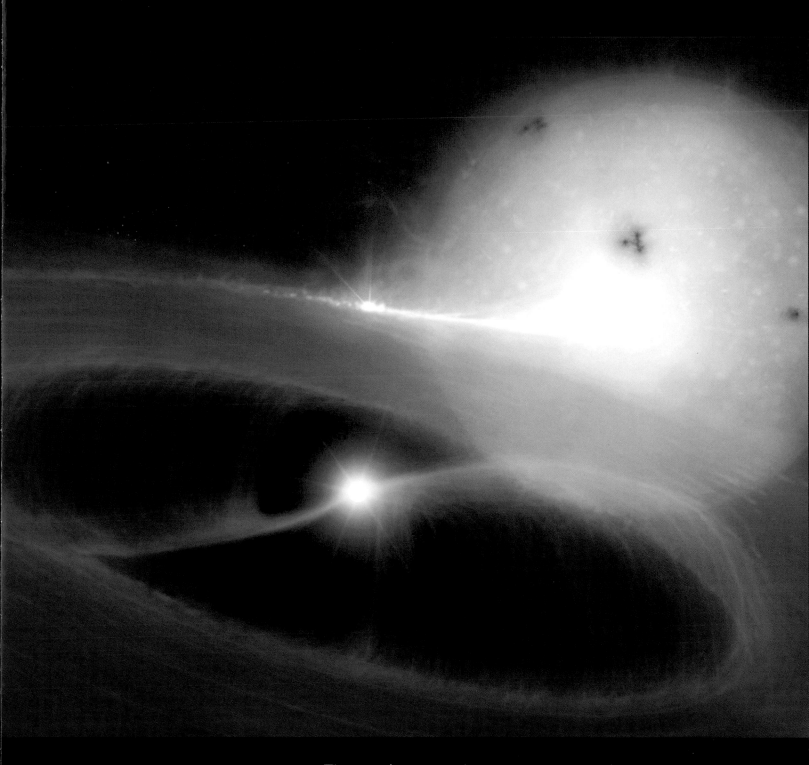

This artist's painting shows gases streaming between two stars.

We soared beyond our galaxy,
and I looked back in time to see
a disc that spiraled out with ease
like lace unraveled in a breeze.

If viewed from above, the Milky Way galaxy would look like a giant
pinwheel spinning through space. Glowing arms of dust, gas, and
stars spiral out from the center. Our Sun lies about halfway out from
the center in one of the spiral arms. Scientists think that the brilliant
white bulge in the middle of the pinwheel is a thick knot of stars,
circling around a black hole.

The Milky Way looks a lot like the Pinwheel galaxy in this photograph.

And when we'd left it far behind,
it was astonishing to find
another, then a hundred more,
each different from the one before.

A galaxy is a huge collection of dust, gas, and billions of stars. Like snowflakes, no two galaxies are alike, but they do come in three basic types. Round or egg-shaped star groups are called elliptical galaxies. Spirals, like the Milky Way, are flattened discs with arms sweeping out from a central bulge. Fuzzy, odd-shaped clumps of stars are called irregular galaxies.

Spiral galaxy from above

Spiral galaxy from the side

Elliptical galaxy

Irregular galaxy

My light steed never ever swerved,

but outer space itself is curved.

So like a bubble in a bath,

I found myself drawn round a path . . .

Light moves through empty space in a straight line, much like a marble rolls straight across a tightly stretched sheet. But rocks dropped on the sheet will create valleys, and the marble will follow the hilly surface up and down. Like the rocks, stars and planets bend space around them, curving it inward toward their centers. And like the marble, a light beam will follow the twists and turns of space.

This computer simulation shows light bending as it follows the curved space around a cluster of galaxies.

Back across the galaxies,

as colorful as coral seas,

to one that spiraled out with ease

like lace unraveled in a breeze.

Galaxies do not spread out evenly through space. They gather in groups, held together by gravity. The Milky Way is one of more than thirty galaxies in the Local Group. At least nine smaller galaxies circle the Milky Way. The closest, the Sagittarius Dwarf galaxy, is actually crashing into our galaxy. Don't worry — it's too small to hurt the Milky Way, and there's so much empty space in both galaxies that it should simply pass on through.

The Andromeda galaxy, pictured here,
looks a lot like our own Milky Way.

Not far beyond a glowing sun
and very near where I'd begun,
I recognized a silver face
that overlooks a special place . . .

As the Moon orbits around Earth, it spins slowly on its axis, always
keeping the same side facing Earth. The other side (the far side) faces
outward toward space. Humans first saw the far side of the Moon
when a robotic probe sent back photographs in 1959. Scientists were
surprised to see that the far side has fewer dark lava plains than the
side that faces Earth. Because the crust is thicker there, it was harder
for molten rock to break through to the surface. So the far side
remains a silvery white.

One graced by water, wind, and air,
to me it never looked so fair —
a bright oasis in the night
inviting me to end my flight.

The first astronauts who traveled to the Moon sent home stunning pictures that revealed the fragile beauty of our world. People everywhere were fascinated by this view of Earth without cultural or political boundaries. For the first time, we saw clearly that all of us share the same precious blue marble, alone in space.

Sailing back to Earth once more
and landing on my sandy shore,
I searched the sky for sparks of light
and knew I'd wonder back one night.

We can't yet sail around the universe, any more than we can travel back in time. But powerful telescopes can show us places far away and long ago. These telescopes gather light that left distant galaxies more than 10 billion years ago, and show us the universe when it was young. One day, astronomers hope to see all the way back to the moment the universe was born, more than 13 billion years ago.

Author's Note

I would not recommend actually taking a trip around the universe, even if you could catch a ride on a light beam. Your round trip would take billions of years. Though you would pass the Sun in eight minutes, it would take four years to reach the nearest star. Traveling at light speed, you would reach the edge of the Milky Way galaxy in 20 thousand years, and it would take 13 billion years to reach some distant galaxies.

Fortunately, however, the universe is coming to us. Light rays from outer space have been traveling our way since the stars began to shine. Today, telescopes around the world, as well as in space, show us all the astounding places pictured in this book, and more.

For additional photographs and information about outer space, visit a nearby planetarium or observatory and explore the following websites:

NASA for Kids
www.nasa.gov/forkids

NASA for Students
www.nasa.gov/audience/forstudents

Astronomy Picture of the Day
http://apod.gsfc.nasa.gov

European Space Agency
www.esa.int/education

The Eight Planets
www.eightplanets.org

Welcome to the Planets
http://pds.jpl.nasa.gov/planets

Interstellar Trip Planner
http://planetquest.jpl.nasa.gov/trip_planner_launch.html

The Universe Forum — Our Place in Space
http://cfa-www.harvard.edu/seuforum/opis_tour_earth.htm

Star Child: A Learning Center for Young Astronomers
http://starchild.gsfc.nasa.gov

Down-to-Earth Astronomy from the Space Telescope Science Institute
www.stsci.edu/outreach

Glossary

atmosphere – The layer of gases surrounding a planet or star. Earth's atmosphere is called air.

atoms – Particles too small to see, that make up all the ordinary matter in the universe.

black hole – A region in space where gravity is so powerful that it traps light and anything else that gets too close.

galaxy – A collection of gas, dust, and billions of stars, all spinning around a common center and held together by gravity.

gravity – The tug or pull of two (or more) objects on each other. Albert Einstein's theory of relativity explains that gravity is caused by the way space curves around matter.

matter – Anything that can be touched. Everything except energy is made up of matter.

nebula – A huge cloud of gas and dust in space. The plural of *nebula* is *nebulae*.

nuclear fusion – The collision of two atoms that results in a single, new atom and the release of energy. When fusion occurs in the Sun's core (center), two hydrogen atoms combine, forming one atom of helium.

planet – A large object that orbits around a star.

solar flare – An explosion of stored energy on the Sun's surface.

solar system – A star and the objects that orbit around it. Our solar system includes the Sun and the nine planets with their moons, as well as millions of asteroids (large rocks) and comets (chunks of ice and rock).

telescope – An instrument used to look at stars and other distant objects. A telescope gathers and magnifies light to make a faraway object look larger and brighter.

twin stars – Two stars that orbit around each other, held together by the pull of gravity. Also called binary stars.

universe – The universe is everything on Earth and in outer space.

To my parents, Thomas and Loyola, who encouraged me to wonder among the stars, and to my sister, Karen, who wondered with me. — J. P.

Special thanks to Dr. Jennifer A. Grier, Educator and Scientist, Harvard-Smithsonian Center for Astrophysics. Many thanks also to Alyssa Mito Pusey for her editorial advice and to Martha MacLeod Sikkema for her design work.

Credits
Front cover: NASA, ESA, and A. Nota (STScI/ESA); Back cover: Barney Magrath; Page 1: Tunç Tezel; Page 3: Chris Cook; Page 5: NOAO / AURA / NSF / WIYN; Page 7: SOHO – EIT Consortium, ESA, NASA; Page 9: Lunar and Planetary Institute, NASA; Page 11: Chris Cook; Page 13: NOAO / AURA / NSF / WIYN; Page 15: Mark Garlick; Page 17: Canada-France-Hawaii Telescope / J.-C. Cuillandre / Coelum; Page 19: Adam Block (KPNO Visitor Program), NOAO, NSF; Page 21: Rychard Bouwens (UCO/Lick Observatory), ACS GTO Team, NASA; Page 23: Robert Gendler; Page 25: Apollo 16, NASA: Page 27: NASA, The Earth Observatory Team — http://earth.observatory.nasa.gov; Page 29: Gemini Observatory photo by Peter Michaud and Kirk Pu'uohau-Pummill; Page 32: NASA

Published by Charlesbridge
85 Main Street
Watertown, MA 02472
(617) 926-0329
www.charlesbridge.com

Library of Congress Cataloging-in-Publication Data
Peddicord, Jane Ann.
Night wonders / Jane Ann Peddicord.
 p. cm.
ISBN-13: 978-1-57091-877-3; ISBN-10: 1-57091-877-5 (reinforced for library use)
ISBN-13: 978-1-57091-878-0; ISBN-10: 1-57091-878-3 (softcover)
1. Solar system—Juvenile literature. 2. Galaxies—Juvenile literature. I. Title.
QB501.3.P44 2005
523dc22   2004010088

Printed in Korea
(hc)   10 9 8 7 6 5 4 3 2
(sc)   10 9 8 7 6 5 4 3 2

The Hubble Space Telescope orbits 380 miles above Earth, taking photographs of deep space.